MARINE SCIENCE IN THE REAL WORLD

by Carol Hand

Content Consultant
Randall Hughes
Assistant Professor of Marine
and Environmental Science
Northeastern University

Core Library

An Imprint of Abdo Publishing
abdopublishing.com

abdopublishing.com

Published by Abdo Publishing, a division of ABDO, PO Box 398166, Minneapolis, Minnesota 55439. Copyright © 2017 by Abdo Consulting Group, Inc. International copyrights reserved in all countries. No part of this book may be reproduced in any form without written permission from the publisher. Core Library™ is a trademark and logo of Abdo Publishing.

Printed in the United States of America, North Mankato, Minnesota
082016
012017

Cover Photo: Alexis Rosenfeld/Science Source
Interior Photos: Alexis Rosenfeld/Science Source, 1; Jeffrey Rotman/Science Source, 4; Louise Murray/Robert Harding/Glow Images, 7; D. Ducros/Science Source, 10, 45; Red Line Editorial, 12, 24; North Wind Picture Archives, 14; Universal History Archive/UIG/Getty Images, 17; Photo12/UIG/Getty Images, 19; Eric Risberg/AP Images, 23; Simon Fraser/Science Source, 26; NOAA-OER/BOEM/US Geological Survey, 29, 43; Spencer Grant/Science Source, 32; NASA, 34; Carl Purcell/Science Source, 36; Alexis Rosenfeld/Science Source, 39

Editor: Arnold Ringstad
Series Designer: Ryan Gale

Publisher's Cataloging-in-Publication Data

Names: Hand, Carol, author.
Title: Marine science in the real world / by Carol Hand.
Description: Minneapolis, MN : Abdo Publishing, 2017. | Series: STEM in the real
    world | Includes bibliographical references and index.
Identifiers: LCCN 2016945467 | ISBN 9781680784800 (lib. bdg.) |
    ISBN 9781680798654 (ebook)
Subjects: LCSH: Aquatic ecology--Juvenile literature. | Marine biology--
    Juvenile literature. | Oceanography--Juvenile literature. | Forensic science--
    Juvenile literature.
Classification: DDC 577.7--dc23
LC record available at http://lccn.loc.gov/2016945467

CONTENTS

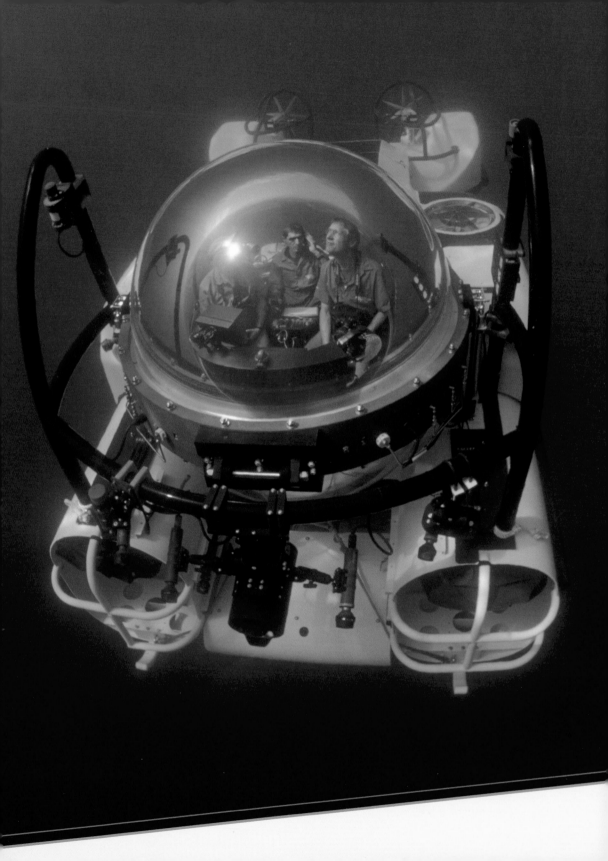

CHAPTER ONE

WHAT IS MARINE SCIENCE?

Dr. Cindy Lee Van Dover is at home on the deep ocean floor. She dives down three miles (4.8 km) in a tiny submersible. The water is completely black. There is no light. It gets colder with every foot of depth. The pressure could crush an unprotected person.

Dr. Van Dover has piloted 48 dives in the submersible *Alvin*. She explores hot springs on the

Submersibles are important tools in the exploration of the deep oceans.

ocean floor. These springs are called hydrothermal vents. They belch water heated by molten volcanic rocks. Dr. Van Dover studies the strange creatures that live nearby. She also sees the effects of humans. She finds lots of trash. There are tracks left by fishing trawlers.

Weird Creatures

Animals around hydrothermal vents are varied and unusual. They include red-tipped tubeworms up to six feet (1.8 m) long. There are shrimp with eyes on their backs. There are ghostly white fish, giant clams, and yellow mussels. There are huge beds of sea anemones. They all live in darkness and crushing pressures. They get heat from deep-sea volcanoes. Bacteria around the vents provide the creatures with energy.

Marine Science and STEM

Dr. Van Dover is a marine scientist. These researchers study oceans. Marine science is also called oceanography. It includes several fields. Marine biologists study ocean plants and animals. Marine geologists study the ocean floor. Marine chemists study the ocean's chemical properties.

Marine scientists use technology to study the ocean environment and its organisms.

Marine physicists study energy in the ocean. They examine things such as heat, light, currents, waves, and tides.

Marine engineers and technologists also play important roles. Marine engineers design submersibles and ships. Marine technologists operate and fix these vehicles. Science, technology, engineering, and math are all involved in these careers. These four subjects are known as STEM.

People in STEM fields usually focus on one area. But they learn about all four STEM areas. Dr. Van Dover studies ocean life, so she is a marine biologist. But she must also know other sciences. She must know technology and engineering to pilot a submersible. She must understand mathematics and computer science too.

What Marine Scientists Study

Oceans cover more than 70 percent of Earth's surface. On maps they are divided into several oceans, including the Atlantic and Pacific. But all of them connect and form one world ocean. Approximately 80 percent of its water volume is deeper than 3,280 feet (1,000 m). Scientists say we know more about the moon and Mars than the deep ocean.

Scientists map the ocean floor. They use radar from satellites and sonar from ships. Radar cannot penetrate the water. It measures differences in the ocean surface. Scientists subtract the effects of waves and tides. Then radar can show mountains and valleys on the ocean floor. More detailed maps are made using sonar. Sonar detects underwater objects. It

IN THE REAL WORLD

The Deepest Dive

James Cameron directed Hollywood movies such as *Avatar*, *Titanic*, and *The Abyss*. He is also an explorer. On March 26, 2012, Cameron visited the deepest point in the ocean. This point is called Challenger Deep. It is located in the Mariana Trench in the western Pacific Ocean. It is 35,800 feet (10,900 m) deep. Cameron piloted the *Deepsea Challenger*, a submersible he helped design. His journey became part of a documentary film called *Deepsea Challenge*.

The TOPEX/Poseidon satellite helped scientists map the oceans from 1992 until 2006.

can measure features approximately 328 feet (100 m) across. By 2016, approximately 10 to 15 percent of the world ocean had been measured to this scale.

Maps show the ocean basin is generally bowl shaped. The part near land is the continental shelf. It drops off steeply to the ocean floor. This drop-off is the continental slope. The deepest part has plains, mountain ranges, valleys, and trenches. Ocean water forms layers that differ in light, temperature, and pressure. Only the shallow sunlight zone at the top has enough light for plants to grow. The next layer down is called the twilight zone. It receives only dim light. No light reaches the midnight zone or abyssal zone. These are the two deepest zones. Below the top layer, the temperature drops rapidly. Pressure increases with depth, as more water presses down from above.

The ocean is vast and deep. Its regions differ widely from each other. Coastal oceans are very different from open oceans. The sunlight zone is very

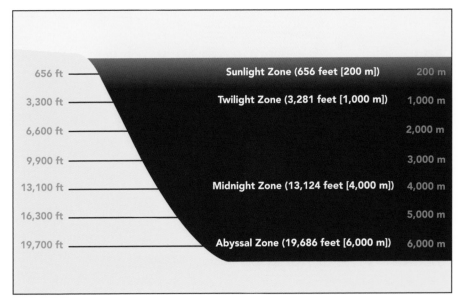

656 ft	Sunlight Zone (656 feet [200 m])	200 m
3,300 ft	Twilight Zone (3,281 feet [1,000 m])	1,000 m
6,600 ft		2,000 m
9,900 ft		3,000 m
13,100 ft	Midnight Zone (13,124 feet [4,000 m])	4,000 m
16,300 ft		5,000 m
19,700 ft	Abyssal Zone (19,686 feet [6,000 m])	6,000 m

Ocean Layers

Most ocean life is in shallow areas around shores and in the sunlit layer. Plants and algae can grow here. This thin, top layer reaches down only to approximately 650 feet (200 m). Below this, it is dark and cold. What types of life, if any, would you expect to find in the midnight and abyssal zones? Suppose you are a marine biologist. What challenges would you face if you wanted to study these regions?

different from the abyssal zone. Scientists seek to understand all parts of the oceans. They are studying how to protect our planet's most important natural resource.

In this 1998 report from the US Department of Commerce, the author describes the importance of ocean exploration:

> *The ocean remains as one of Earth's last unexplored frontiers. It has stirred our imaginations over the millennia and has led to the discovery of new lands, immense deposits and reservoirs of resources, and startling scientific findings. The presence of the human eye and the human ability to sample and to conduct experiments from the coastal regions to the deep ocean abyss has provided answers to questions on such critical issues as global change, waste disposal, mineral deposits, and the creation of life itself. In spite of the development of new technologies, comparatively little of the ocean has been studied. . . . [P]ublic opinion polls . . . indicate that ocean exploration is more important than space studies. As exciting and enlightening as ocean discoveries have been, they will pale in comparison to future discoveries.*
>
> Source: "Ocean Explorer." NOAA. NOAA, February 8, 2013. Web. Accessed April 13, 2016.

Consider Your Audience

This summary was written for members of the US Congress. Rewrite the text for your fellow students. How did you change the text, and why?

CHAPTER TWO

THE HISTORY OF MARINE SCIENCE

The Polynesians began exploring the Pacific Ocean by 4000 BCE. The Phoenicians and Greeks explored the Mediterranean Sea between 2000 and 400 BCE. Between 700 and 1000 CE, the Vikings explored the North Atlantic Ocean. The Vikings reached Iceland, Greenland, and even North America. All of these explorers

The Vikings were among the civilizations that became experts in sea exploration.

understood tides, winds, ocean currents, and weather. They were pioneering marine scientists.

Ocean Discovery and Scientific Expeditions

The Age of Discovery lasted from 1400 CE through the early 1900s. Adventurers sailed the seas in large ships. They mapped the oceans and made new discoveries. Military voyagers claimed new territory. Many European countries led voyages. Famous explorers included Christopher Columbus, Ferdinand Magellan, and James Cook.

The Age of Scientific Expeditions began in the 1800s. One of the earliest scientific voyages was the US Exploring Expedition (1829–1843). It traveled 90,000 miles (145,000 km). The crew charted Pacific islands and the coast of Antarctica.

On the Challenger Expedition (1872–1876), scientists discovered many new species. They located the deepest part of the ocean, the Mariana Trench. In 1968, the Glomar Challenger Expedition studied

The Challenger Expedition made observations at hundreds of sites around the world's oceans.

ocean floor processes. Its researchers used a specially built drilling rig.

Marine labs were developed to study ocean specimens. They became centers for marine research. The first US marine lab was the University of California's Scripps Institution of Oceanography. It was founded in 1903. Woods Hole Oceanographic Institution (WHOI) in Massachusetts was founded in 1930. These and other labs have discovered many new marine species.

Diving Suits and Submersibles

As marine science advanced, people developed technology to explore the oceans. This included diving suits and submersibles. Such equipment allowed divers to stay underwater longer. It provided air and protected divers from intense pressures.

The word *scuba* originally stood for "self-contained underwater breathing apparatus." The technology has been used since 1825. Early divers discovered that surfacing too quickly causes

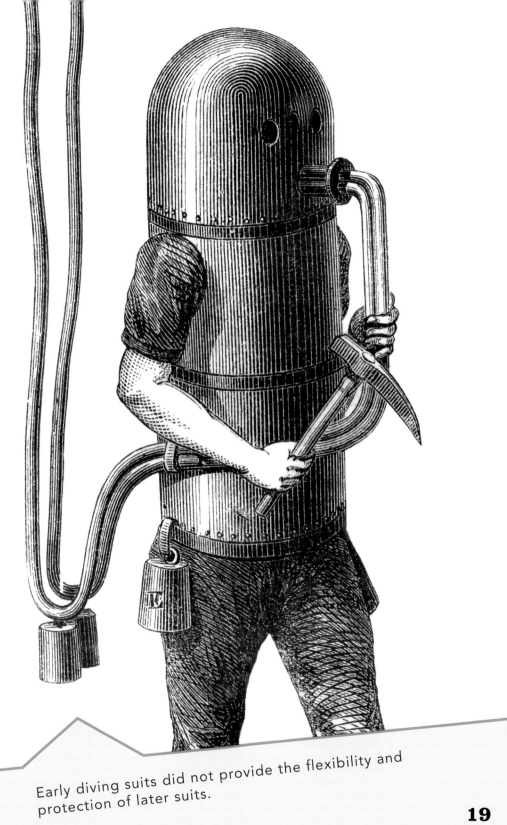

Early diving suits did not provide the flexibility and protection of later suits.

a condition called the bends. Dissolved gases form bubbles in the blood as divers rise. This causes illness or death. Surfacing slowly allows divers to avoid these effects. In 1907, British scientist John Scott Haldane developed a set of mathematical tables to help divers surface safely. His decompression tables list many diving depths. They show the time it takes for lungs to return to normal pressures from each depth.

A breakthrough came in 1943. Jacques Cousteau

and Emile Gagnan invented the aqualung. This was the first scuba equipment that adjusted air pressure. It supplied air when the diver needed it. It included a safety valve. The valve matched the diver's lung pressure to the water pressure. However, scuba divers must still surface slowly. Otherwise, they suffer from the bends.

Jacques Cousteau, Ocean Pioneer

Jacques Cousteau was a French ocean explorer, researcher, and photographer. He coinvented the aqualung. He also developed an underwater camera. Cousteau is most famous for scientific voyages. These were shown on a television series called *The Undersea World of Jacques Cousteau.* Cousteau introduced millions of people to the wonders of the ocean.

Submarines and Submersibles

Underwater vehicles are built to protect people. They withstand high pressures and low temperatures. People inside can breathe normally. The two main types of underwater vehicles are submersibles and submarines. Submersibles are small and used for scientific research. Submarines are much larger. They are used for warfare. The earliest submarines were hand powered. Later submarines used diesel engines. Many submarines today are powered by nuclear reactors. The US Navy developed nuclear submarines in the 1950s.

In the 1960s, engineers built submersibles for scientific use. *Alvin* was built for the US Navy. It holds three people and dives to 12,000 feet (3,700 m). It has lights, cameras, and two robotic arms. Its basket can hold up to 400 pounds (180 kg) of samples. *Alvin* was the first submersible to explore Pacific hydrothermal vents. It provided early glimpses of the wreck of the *Titanic*. This famous ship sank in 1912. *Alvin* is now operated by the WHOI. By 2016 it had made more than 4,700 dives. *Alvin* is the world's oldest submersible. It is continually upgraded and inspected.

Today, deep-ocean researchers also use robotic vehicles. They have used remotely operated vehicles (ROVs) since the 1970s. ROVs are remote controlled.

The DeepWorker 2000 submersible holds only one person.

The DeepWorker Submersible	
Length	10 feet (3.1 m)
Beam (width)	6 feet (1.8 m)
Height	5.75 feet (1.75 m)
Weight in air	2.75 tons (2.50 metric tons)
Operating depth	3,300 feet (1,000 m)
Payload (weight carried)	250 pounds (113 kg)
Life support system	80 hours
Maximum speed	3 knots (3.5 miles per hour, 5.6 km/h)
Passengers	1 person (pilot)

Submersible Specifications

DeepWorker is a single-passenger submersible. It is compact, lightweight, and easy to operate. The passenger acts as pilot, researcher, and camera operator. Study the table giving information about DeepWorker. If you were exploring the deep ocean, what advantages would DeepWorker have? How would it be better than scuba gear or a diving suit?

They provide a stable platform for cameras and lighting systems. Autonomous underwater vehicles (AUVs) move without human control. They perform simple tasks on their own. For example, they watch for biological changes on the seabed.

Sylvia Earle is a marine biologist and explorer. She described what she sees as the present and future of the oceans:

> Fisheries including swordfish, cod, tuna, and salmon have collapsed or are on the verge of doing so, and many of our coastal regions are polluted, overdeveloped, or eroding. Whales and dolphins are increasingly washing ashore dead or dying. Coral reefs, one of the most spectacular and diverse environments on the planet, are showing global signs of ill health, yet some continue to be fished ruthlessly with cyanide, bleach, and dynamite. And, a marine "dead zone" has developed off the Mississippi delta in the Gulf of Mexico, and may mean the permanent destruction of an underwater area the size of New Jersey. The key to preventing further degradation of the ocean and protecting—maybe even restoring—it for future generations lies in our understanding of the sea and our ability to manage our impact on it.

Source: Ellen J. Prager with Sylvia Earle. *The Oceans*. New York: McGraw-Hill, 2000. Print. x.

Back It Up

The author is using evidence to support a point. Write a short paragraph describing the point the author is making. Then write down two or three pieces of evidence the author uses to make the point.

CHAPTER THREE

CAREERS IN MARINE SCIENCE

Most marine scientists spend little time at sea. Many work most of the year in classrooms or laboratories. They take one or two long research cruises a year. They may also use small vessels to explore areas closer to shore. They bring back samples and data to study. Marine scientists usually focus on one type of science.

Marine scientists often spend much of their time in laboratories.

But scientists of all kinds work together and share information.

The Variety of Marine Sciences

Marine physicists often use remote sensing. This involves studying things from far away. Remote sensing can be used to study ocean currents. It can measure water temperatures. It can track changes in sea ice. Dr. Bob Embley is a geophysicist with the National Oceanic and Atmospheric Administration (NOAA). He studies undersea volcanoes. He analyzes seafloor data using computers. Dr. Embley has also led undersea expeditions. He has seen undersea landslides and volcanic eruptions.

Dr. Sandra Brooke is a marine biologist. She studies coral reefs in deep ocean canyons. She works to pass laws to protect ocean ecosystems. Dr. Brooke enjoys seeing the amazing life on the ocean floor.

Jennifer McClain-Counts has a master's degree in marine science. She manages a chemical laboratory for the US Geological Survey. She studies nitrogen in

McClain-Counts, left, gets ready to study a sample taken from the Atlantic Ocean.

marine organisms. This shows her each animal's place in the food web.

Skills and Preparation

Marine scientists must be well trained in STEM areas. They also need excellent writing and speaking skills. The scientists write articles about their data. Then they present these articles at conferences. They must talk to many kinds of people. They work long hours.

Young people can prepare for a marine science career long before college. They should take science and math courses in high school. They should learn to work well in groups. They should read books about marine science. And they should also visit the coast whenever possible.

Successful marine scientists need laboratory and field experience. Students in high school should look for these opportunities. They can find a part-time job or internship in a lab, aquarium, or fish hatchery.

Education for Marine Science

Marine science careers require a college degree. People with bachelor's

Oceans and Plastics Pollution

Tomorrow's marine scientists must deal with ocean pollution. The north Pacific Ocean contains a swirling mass of garbage. This patch of trash is twice the size of Texas. Ocean currents have gathered it into a single area. Much of it is made up of plastic. Fish and seabirds die from eating plastic. Sea turtles, seals, dolphins, and whales become tangled in plastic ropes, fishing lines, and nets.

degrees may work in labs. They work under professors or senior researchers. Most jobs require graduate degrees, either master's degrees or PhDs. Professors and leaders of research groups must have a PhD.

Undergraduate students can study a major branch of science, such as biology, chemistry, physics, or geology. They can take marine science courses within this branch. Graduate students specialize further. They study subjects such as marine biology or marine geology.

As with marine scientists, students interested in ocean

IN THE REAL WORLD

Standing on the Seafloor

Diver Graham Hawkes described what it is like to stand on the bottom of the Atlantic Ocean in a diving suit:

> One of the things that's very different from scuba is that you're breathing normally and there are no bubbles. You are very aware of your breath. . . . There is no splashing. . . . It just felt like I was standing on an alien planet.

Students test a small ROV they designed and built.

conservation must know science. But they might major in environmental studies or wildlife conservation. Like traditional science majors, they can choose courses on marine topics. Many colleges offer such majors. Students should check each college's courses and programs to find those that fit them best.

EXPLORE ONLINE

Visit the website below for NOAA's Southwest Fisheries Science Center. Read the section on Careers in Marine Biology. Compare the information on this website with the information in this chapter about careers in marine science. What additional information did you get from the website?

Careers in Marine Biology

mycorelibrary.com/marine-science

CHAPTER FOUR

THE FUTURE OF MARINE SCIENCE

No matter where we live, oceans affect us all. They contain 97 percent of Earth's water. Their plants produce half the planet's oxygen. They absorb some of the carbon dioxide that causes climate change. They regulate weather. They contain strange and wonderful life-forms. They provide food, medicines, jobs, and recreation.

Oceans cover most of Earth, and they are critical to life on the planet.

Workers nurse a sea turtle back to health in Florida.

Marine scientists continue to explore and study this vast, mysterious world. They learn what the ocean contains and how it works. They study the ocean from its surface to its greatest depths. Many are trying to preserve the oceans and their resources. New technologies will aid all this work. Scientists will use computer models, satellite data, and infrared imaging. Submersibles will allow more scientists to study the undersea world in person.

Dangers to the Oceans

People may think oceans are so big that we cannot harm them. But there are many threats to the world's oceans. People have already overfished many marine fisheries. The oceans are used as highways to ship goods between continents. This leads to waste dumping. Drilling for oil, gas, and minerals damages the seafloor. It causes major pollution problems, including oil spills. And climate change is a looming threat. These combined dangers may lead to a massive extinction of ocean life.

Oceans and Climate Change

Climate change raises ocean temperatures and increases acidity. Warmer oceans contain more energy. This causes stronger hurricanes. Melting ice raises sea levels. Warming waters expand, raising sea levels even further. This will worsen flooding and the loss of coastal land. Increasing acidity makes it harder for corals and shellfish to build skeletons and shells. Scientists agree that if current trends continue, the future of coral reefs is in danger.

Many scientists will concentrate on how oceans function. They might study the oceans' effects on climate. They might study ocean fisheries or phytoplankton. These are the tiny floating algae that provide food for all ocean life. Those in marine conservation will tackle ocean dangers directly. They will work to save individual species, such as fish, dolphins, or sea turtles. They will work on coral reefs or Arctic ecosystems. They will seek ways to make ocean drilling safer. And they will clean up after oil spills.

Future Ocean Technologies

Modern ROVs and submersibles have better sensors than ever before. They are stronger and more capable too. The ROV *Deep Discoverer* can handle depths of nearly 4 miles (6.4 km) and pressures 600 times those at sea level. Another ROV called *ROPOS* carries out scientific activities at depths to 3.1 miles (5 km). The two-part system *Jason/Medea* can reach 4 miles (6.4 km) below the surface. *Jason* and *Medea* are

ROVs are often lowered into the water from much larger ships.

tethered together. They can do wide surveys of the ocean floor.

Many new submersibles have also been developed. *Mir I* and *II* are two recent submersibles. These vessels are battery powered. They carry three people each. The submersibles dive to about 3.8 miles (6.1 km). They can reach almost 98 percent of the ocean floor. New ROVs and submersibles are opening up the undersea world.

Moving Forward

There is great competition for marine science jobs. People who want to become marine scientists will need strong skills in science. They will also need mathematics and computer science to get the jobs of their dreams. Today's talented students will become the next generation of marine scientists. The future of our planet's oceans may be in their hands.

FURTHER EVIDENCE

In the below article, seven people describe their vision of the world oceans in 2050. Review the information in this chapter. Identify the chapter's main point. List supporting evidence for that point. Find a quotation on the website that either supports the evidence in the chapter or adds new evidence.

The Future of Oceans
mycorelibrary.com/marine-science

- Marine scientists, or oceanographers, study anything to do with the oceans. They may specialize in marine biology, ecology, geology, chemistry, or physics.
- Most marine science positions require a master's degree or PhD. Students often get a bachelor's degree in a core science and specialize in a marine science in graduate school.
- Marine scientists need excellent communication and writing skills, computer and technology skills, and field and laboratory skills.
- Marine science jobs are highly competitive. Employers include governments, universities, marine research stations, conservation organizations, and private industries, such as the oil and gas industry.
- The first ocean voyages were undertaken for exploration or military purposes. In the 1800s, scientific explorers began to map the oceans and shores and identify sea life.

- Scuba gear and diving suits were developed to explore the ocean's depths. This equipment protects divers and allows them to remain underwater for several hours at a time.
- Submersibles are self-contained and hold one or a few people. They dive several miles into the ocean. These vessels allow people to view and sample undersea life.
- ROVs and AUVs are vehicles that can study the ocean floor while scientists remain on the surface. ROVs are controlled remotely. AUVs move independently.

Take a Stand

In Chapter Four, you learned that the oceans are at risk from pollution, climate change, overharvesting, and other dangers. You also learned that some people are developing ways to live underwater. Do you think people should colonize the oceans? Or do you think this would cause even greater damage? Why?

Another View

In Chapter One, you read that we know more about the surfaces of the moon and Mars than we know about the deep ocean. As you know, every source is different. Ask an adult to help you find another source about how much we know about the deep ocean. Write a short essay comparing and contrasting the new source's point of view with that of this book's author. What is the point of view of each author? How are they similar and why? How are they different and why?

Tell the Tale

In Chapter One, you learned about the various layers of the ocean. Imagine you are diving down through the ocean. Write 200 words about what you see as you move downward. How does the environment change?

Surprise Me

Chapter Three deals with becoming a marine scientist. After reading this book and learning about careers in marine science, what two or three facts about these careers did you find most surprising? Write a few sentences about each fact. Why did you find each fact surprising?

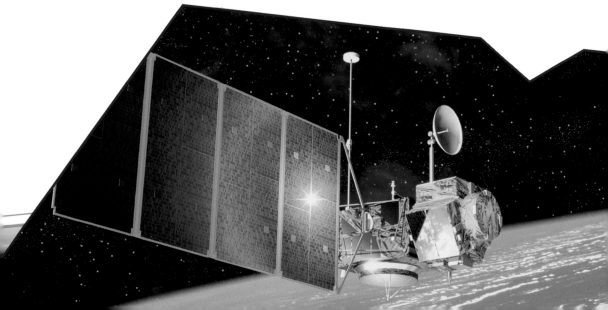

GLOSSARY

aquanaut
a person who lives in an underwater shelter

decompression
the process by which a diver returns slowly to the surface after a deep dive, so the lungs can return to normal surface pressure

extinction
the complete disappearance, or dying out, of a species

hydrothermal vent
an opening on the deep ocean floor from which molten volcanic material erupts; vents can support many living creatures

radar
a system for detecting distant objects using radio waves

scuba
a self-contained underwater breathing apparatus; scuba gear consists of a tank of compressed air attached by tubes to a face mask and delivered to the diver at a safe pressure

sonar
a system for measuring depth or detecting underwater objects

submersible
an underwater vehicle holding one or a few people, used for scientific research

LEARN MORE

Books

MacQuitty, Miranda. *Eyewitness Ocean*. New York: DK Publishing, 2014.

Mara, Wil. *Deep-Sea Exploration*. New York: Children's Press, 2015.

Webb, Sophie. *Far from Shore: Chronicles of an Open Ocean Voyage*. Boston, MA: HMH Books for Young Readers, 2011.

Websites

To learn more about STEM in the Real World, visit **booklinks.abdopublishing.com**. These links are routinely monitored and updated to provide the most current information available.

Visit **mycorelibrary.com** for free additional tools for teachers and students.

INDEX

ABOUT THE AUTHOR

Carol Hand has written more than 30 science and technology books for young people. She has a PhD in marine biology. She is very concerned about marine environmental problems, including plastics pollution and climate change.

DATE DUE

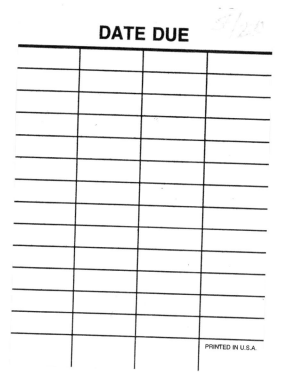

PRINTED IN U.S.A.